Contents

Getting started...
Your checklist for a happy healthy pet

[ ] **Hutch/indoor cage & run**
[ ] **Ceramic food bowl**
[ ] **Water bottle**
[ ] **Woodshavings**
[ ] **Hay**
[ ] **Guinea pig nuggets**
[ ] **Mineral stone**
[ ] **Vitamin supplement**
[ ] **Probiotic supplement**
[ ] **Treats**
[ ] **Toys with hideaway holes**
[ ] **Bottle brush**
[ ] **Brush/ comb**
[ ] **Gnawing sticks**
[ ] **Cage disinfectant**

Useful books

[✓] **Good Pet Guide: The Guinea pig**
[ ] **Pet Friendly: Guinea pigs**

Introduction

1. Guinea pig

Guinea pigs, or Cavies *(Latin: Cavia porcellus)* **are one of the most popular of the pet rodents.**

Their cute faces and vocalizations make them an instant hit with all age groups and their size and shape allow them to be handled easily by children. In addition to their robust build and gracious attitude, they are well known for being slightly neurotic but wonderfully lovable creatures.

They are the perfect choice for the beginner pet owner. Guinea pigs are generally gentle little creatures and will soon become tame if kept in contact with humans from a young age. They do not climb their cage, as they are not as agile as hamsters or gerbils, and as such, they prove to be less trouble if they do manage to escape.

Guinea pigs are ideal house pets but are often kept outside in hutches. This is acceptable, but as they are comfortable in a similar temperature range as humans, it is usually much better if they can be kept indoors, especially during the winter months. They will quickly get accustomed to the busy surroundings and get on well with other household pets if introduced properly *(introductions should only be through the bars of their enclosure, as a pet dog or cat may not distinguish between your guinea pig and a wild animal and may harm them if left unattended or in the open).*

Guinea pigs are almost odor free *(if their home is cleaned regularly, p17),* they are cheap to maintain, cheap to feed, easy to handle and will almost never bite. They are a great all round pet and given the correct treatment *(as outlined in this book)* they will genuinely thrive in a loving environment and be a great addition to the family.

Did you know?
A Guinea Pig is
NOT a pig!

2. Origins & habitat

The guinea pig originated in South America and is a descendant of the *restless cavy*. So named because they are known to sleep with their eyes open.

Domesticated around 5000 BC for food by tribes in the Andean region *(present-day Ecuador, Peru and Bolivia)*. To this day they are still bred as a source of food called *'Cur,'* with many households in the region keeping guinea pigs for their fur and as a food source. It is also traditional in these parts to give a newly married couple a breeding pair of guinea pigs as a gift.

In the wild they live in big family groups in the long grasses, seeking protection from predators in the camouflage that this provides. Guinea pigs are not traditionally burrowing animals, instead they tend to occupy the abandoned burrows dug by other animals.

Early traders brought us the guinea pig to Europe and the U.S in the late 1800s and it wasn't long before people fell in love with them. They soon became hugely popular as exotic pets among royalty and the upper classes and selective breeding created many varieties from which most of the breeds we know today have descended.

Many people believe that they got the name *'guinea pig'* because sailors at the time would sell them for one guinea and because they make squeaking noises similar to a pig.

The only other credible theory is that it is a corruption of the word *'Guiana'* from the Dutch port of Guiana, where the animals were exported. Even though both explanations seem plausible, proof is lacking to substantiate either, so it may always remain a bit of a mystery.

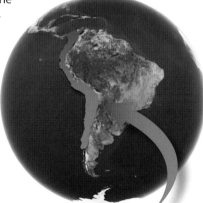

ANDES REGION, SOUTH AMERICA

Top tips

A must have...

→ A home
→ Wood shavings
→ Bedding
→ Water bottle
→ Food bowls
→ Food

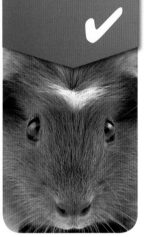

3. Life span

Guinea pigs can live between 4- 7 years.

Age isn't really an important factor when buying a guinea pig as a pet. But you should ensure that your new pet is over 8 weeks old. At this age a guinea pig pup will have been weaned off from the mother and be readily eating solid foods.

Perfect pet?

4. Great pets

Guinea pigs enjoy exploring their environments. They are generally happy, inquisitive and lively little pets. This is why the guinea pig is such a popular pet today in so many countries worldwide.

They make especially good pets for those at work or school during the day. Guinea pigs tend to be less active during the daytime and provided that they are given the right companionship, they are happy to be left alone during this period.

Guinea pigs are sociable animals and need the company and security of other guinea pigs, especially if the owner is away during the daytime or your guinea pig is kept in an outdoor hutch. Rabbits however do not make an ideal hutch mate as their dietary needs are slightly different to that of the guinea pig, as well as the obvious size differences.

5. How many?

Guinea pigs are very social creatures and it is best to keep multiple guinea pigs together.

As pack animals they will be very lonely on their own and this can lead to health and behavior problems. Keeping mixed gender groups can also cause problems as they will tend to breed, so to reduce problems when keeping multiple guinea pigs, always choose pets of the same sex.

In the wild, guinea pigs live in close family colonies. When kept as pets, their instincts are still much the same, and where possible they should be housed together. This ensures that their living conditions are as natural as possible. You should not deprive your pet from the company of other guinea pigs. For example, if you keep you guinea pigs outside, then a group of guinea pigs will be able to survive colder weather more easily as they will huddle together sharing body heat, whereas a lone guinea pig will almost certainly have problems and could suffer from exposure *(which can be fatal)*. To further prevent the danger of exposure you should make sure that the hutch always has sufficient dry bedding and that the hutch is free from drafts *(see p8)*.

You can keep multiple female guinea pigs *(sows)* together, they normally get on well together and will thrive on the company *(just ensure you have enough space)*. However, boars are slightly different. Adult males may fight with each other if they have not been kept together from a young age, and even if they have, it isn't advisable that you keep more than two together as this will often cause problems.

Varieties

Guinea pigs have been successfully bred by skilled breeders for many years and now there are more than 25 different breeds all with varying colors and markings. They can be found in short, long and rough haired varieties, even hairless guinea pigs have been bred. Below are a few of the most popular breeds:

6. Tortoiseshell and white

This popular breeds coat is covered with blocks of color of roughly equal proportions. Black and red *(tortoiseshell)*, or black, red and white *(tortoiseshell and white)*.

7. Himalayan

Marked much like Siamese cats, however the coloration does not become defined *(around the ears, nose and feet)* until the guinea pig is five or six months old.

8. Short-haired breeds

The so-called **Teddies** *(Rex)* with short curled/ fuzzy hair, satin with its trademark sheen or self breeds *(see Top tip above)* are the easiest of all to groom, generally with smooth short coats that bear resemblance to their wild counterparts.

9. Rough-haired breeds

Abyssinian are the most common of rough-haired breeds. Their hair forms easily recognizable whirl patterns across the body. Pure breeds should have ten whirls in total, four on the back end, four around the *'saddle'* and a further one on each of its shoulders, these in particular can push the hair on their face forward giving the impression that they have sideburns and a *quiff*. They appear in a range of different colors.

10. Long-haired breeds

The most well known of these is the **Peruvian** which have long, silky hair similar in design to that of the **Abyssinian**, though very long, usually reaching the floor, leaving them to peek out from behind a mass of hair. They require regular grooming to keep them clean and tidy. Other well known varieties of long hair guinea pigs are, the **Sheltie** *(long straight hair)*, the **Texel** *(a rex coated variant of the sheltie)* and the lesser known **Merino** *(again, like the sheltie but with a slight crimped effect to their coats)*.

11. Agouti

This breed closely resemble wild cavies and has a coat similar to that of a wild rabbit in coloration. The hairs are tipped with a lighter shade than the rest of the hair giving the effect of a shiny coat. There are gold, silver, salmon, lemon and cinnamon agoutis.

12. Mixed breed

These tend to live longer, healthier lives then pedigrees who by definition are subject to inbreeding, and have access to a limited gene pool which can result in health problems. Mixed breeds more varied mix of genes are generally healthier.

Choosing your guinea pig

13. Male or female?

Female guinea pigs are called sows and male guinea pigs are called boars.

The two pictures and instructions below should help when you are sexing your guinea pig. If you have any doubts, the store staff can confirm your guinea pig's sex for you.

Male *(boar)*   Female *(sow)*

The left shows the boar *(male)* while the right shows the sow. Notice that on the boar, the penis is completely retractable only leaving a raised ring *(this is clearly visible by the time the boar reaches maturity at around 6 weeks)*. With the sow it is a typical 'Y' formation that will show the female genitalia.

Even pet shop owners can make mistakes with the sex of the guinea pig so it is usually a good idea to have a double check before purchasing.

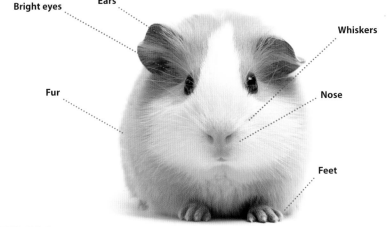

Bright eyes

Ears

Whiskers

Fur

Nose

Feet

14. Know your guinea pig

Ensure that the pet you choose is active and interested in its surroundings, has a glossy coat, clean ears, bright eyes, and a well rounded body free of bumps or swellings. **Below are a few points to consider when choosing your guinea pig:**

→ Mouth

The mouth should have no signs of dribbling or scabbing at the corners *(this can be a sign of a fungal infection)*.

→ Eyes

Should be bright and alert with no sign of discharge or cloudiness. If they look dull it could be sign of a more serious health issue, check regularly for foreign bodies.

→ Ears

The ears are hairless, upright or drooping depending on the variety of guinea pig and varying in size. Their hearing however is much better than ours. A small amount of wax in the ear is normal but if more than this is present it should be cleaned out.

→ Teeth

A guinea pig's teeth constantly grow and are called *'open rooted'*. In total, a guinea pig has 20 teeth and the incisor teeth should be white.

→ Nose

Make sure the nose is clean, there shouldn't be any mucus in or around the nose.

→ Lack of tail

The tail does not come outside the body, but there are 8 tailbones that can be felt under the skin.

→ Attitude/ personality

A guinea pig should show a normal *(not flattened)* posture, have a healthy appetite and sharp, lively reactions *(a lethargic guinea pig is one that isn't in peak condition)*.

→ Paws

Each front paw has four claws. The back feet have three claws. Ensure that the individual toes are straight and supple.

→ Hair

If the hair around the guinea pig's anus is matted, it could mean the guinea pig is suffering from diarrhoea. It should have a glossy but not greasy coat with no bald patches.

→ Hiding

It's the common view that a pet that runs to you wanting attention is the one that you should opt for. But with guinea pigs it is the opposite response. A guinea pig that bolts quickly and hides is showing you that it's a healthy, sprightly animal with a nervous system that is working well. However, It will get used to you quickly once home with you and it will no longer see you as a threat.

Housing your guinea pig

1.

Chewing cables

If you do keep your guinea pig indoors, keep all cables out of reach. This will allow your guinea pig to roam freely without causing damage to itself or your electrics.

15. Outdoors

If an outdoor hutch is used, extra insulation is usually needed as guinea pigs require warmer conditions than a rabbit would. Hideaways and extra hay bedding is essential in the colder months.

The hutch should ideally be kept inside the house but a shed, garage or porch will suffice. By doing this, the hutch is kept out of the elements and will minimize risk to your pets' health. There should always be a secure bedding area in the hutch that contains dry bedding, this area should also be draft free but still provide ventilation.

If you can't keep your hutch out of the elements then you must ensure that the hutch is properly insulated against wind, rain and damp. You can purchase a *'Hutch Hugger'* which will protect the hutch and your guinea pig against bad weather *(available from most pet stores)*. You should ensure that your guinea pigs home is a safe environment for your pet, safe from animals getting in as well as preventing your guinea pig escaping.

16. Indoors

Guinea pigs are comfortable in the same temperature range as humans, so indoor housing is a good idea, there are fewer considerations when doing this, and it will make bonding with your pet easier as you will find that your pet will be more tame from regular human contact.

Even guinea pigs that are housed in outdoor hutches need to come indoors from time to time. When the weather outside means that your outdoor *run* or *grazing area* cannot be used, it is still important that your guinea pig can exercise. As their native name *'restless cavy'* suggests, they require daily exercise and leaving them locked up for long periods is not advised. They will be quite happy exploring inside the home. Just ensure that all cables are out of reach, that other animals are supervised and it has a suitable bolt hole to hide in should it get scared *(upturned cardboard boxes make good little hideaways)*.

17. Introducing to the hutch

You should be prepared and have your guinea pigs hutch set up fully before the arrival of your guinea pig, preferably have it set up for a day before its arrival.

Let them roam freely to begin with to explore their new surroundings. Try not to pick your new pet up for a few days to let them get accustomed to their new home and to you. Speak softly to your guinea pig and try to use their name frequently.

Once they are used to their new home, be careful to acclimatize them to human contact slowly. Start by stroking your guinea pig with one finger while they are roaming and eating in their run. Next, start using the full hand, then occasionally lifting it *(see p18)*, until such a time as it is comfortable with you and with being held.

(see p18)

Top tips

Size of run

Size of the run will depend on the number of guinea pigs you have. But as a rule, the bigger the better as this will give them an interesting environment in which to roam. Try to let them out of their run for a roam about in the room where you spend the most time at least once a day.

✔

18. Hidey holes

Guinea pigs love hiding in small spaces stuffed with soft, dry hay. This type of hiding place simulates the same feeling of security that they would have in their wild habitats.

All guinea pigs should have a structure in their cage to hide in *(this helps to satisfy their instinct to flee when they feel threatened)*, either a wooden hidey hole or woven bedding area will provide enough of a snug environment to make them feel safe. These are also used to chew on *(guinea pigs need to chew regularly to keep their teeth worn down).*

19. Outdoor runs & enclosures

Outside of the colder months your guinea pig may have a wire mesh enclosure, often referred to as a *run,* attached to it via a ramp so that the hutch space can be extended out onto a lawn.

This gives your guinea pig more chance to explore their surroundings and make the most of the warmth and soft summer breezes. Guinea pigs also act as great lawn mowers and they will ensure that your garden is kept trim. However, at night your pet should always be shut into the main hutch area with a catch or bolt, especially if there is a danger of attack from wild animals.

Young Children

Young children must always be supervised when with their guinea pigs.

2. Guinea pig run. Larger rabbit runs are also suitable.

2.

The guinea pig food guide

20. Food glorious food

Each guinea pig will have different likes and dislikes, like we do, when it comes to food.

It is important to know what you can and can not feed your guinea pig to avoid harming it and to help make sure it is receiving all the nutrients that it needs to stay healthy. In their natural environment their diet would mainly consist of grasses and seeds, therefore in captivity you should try to simulate this diet as closely as possible.

Guinea pigs, like all herbivores, require the long indigestible fibre in grass and hay for their unique digestive systems; it also helps to keep their teeth under control and at the correct length.

They should have an unlimited supply of hay and can live quite happily on a diet of good quality hay, pure dried grass, wild plants/herbs and vegetables. However, you should always provide a staple diet feed for your little pets and plenty of fresh water.

21. Pellets

Specially made pellets (*alfalfa*) just for guinea pigs are the mainstay of a healthy guinea pig's diet.

When used in conjunction with the fresh foods *(as listed opposite, No. 23)* they can be used to good effect to provide a well balanced nutritious diet. Another benefit with pellet food is that it restricts your guinea pigs from *selective feeding,* where the animals eats its favorite foods and leaves the rest.

22. Hay

Guinea pigs should always have access to a constant supply of hay.

Grass hay such as **oat, timothy** or **meadow** hay is essential to their digestion and is a large percentage of what they eat. You should supplement this with any good guinea pig mix and fresh vegetables for a well rounded healthy diet. It is important that any hay you use is dry, clean and mold free.

Alfalfa hay *(a legume hay)* has higher protein, calcium and carbohydrates and should be fed to young pups, pregnant and nursing cavies.

1.

2.

1. Sweetcorn
2. Avoid feeding potato

23. Good foods

Good foods for guinea pigs include:

Cauliflower leaves (but not the white 'flower') | broccoli florets | purple sprouting broccoli | green or black cabbage | kale | chicory | carrots | parsnips | sweetcorn | raw beetroot | celery | cucumber | parsley | spring greens | basil | spinach

Good wild plants include:

Golden rod | cleavers | yarrow | dandelion (given sparingly as dandelion is a diuretic) | mallow | shepherds purse

Bad foods/ plants:

Potato | rhubarb | tomato leaves | daffodil | tulip | lily of the valley | lettuce

Milk & dairy!

Milk and yoghurt foods made for humans or other pets should not be given to a guinea pig as they are lactose intolerant.

24. Vitamin C

Guinea pigs cannot produce vitamin C in their bodies and need a fresh supply in their diet daily.

Green leafy vegetables like broccoli and cabbage contain this essential vitamin. Fresh and dried grass and special supplement pellets are sold especially for the guinea pigs specific need for vitamin C.

25. Treats

Special treats include melon or a stick of celery which will be dragged away hastily into cover for solitary consumption, away from troublesome friends.

Fresh fruits are ideal such as oranges, apples, pears, strawberries, melons and tomatoes as well as carrots *(which are a firm guinea pig favorite even though they aren't fruit).*

Top tips

Feeding tips

Wash the guinea pigs food dish out every day to prevent the spread of bacteria.

Use specially formulated guinea pig pellets.

Give them greens daily because of their vitamin C deficiency.

Stick to a feeding routine. Twice a day usually, once in the morning and once in the evening.

Keep water topped up at all times

26. Water

The amount of water a guinea pig needs will vary so it is always advisable that you have an constant supply of water within easy reach of your pet whether it in the house, hutch or grazing in its enclosure.

The water should be available in a bottle instead of a bowl. A bowl will quickly become soiled and unhealthy for you pet to drink.

Play time

27. Exercise

Guinea pigs will benefit greatly from being kept in good shape. Well exercised guinea pigs will live longer and have fewer health problems.

As with humans, guinea pigs can experience similar health problems that arise as a result of being overweight. They will have higher tendencies for heart disease, diabetes, bladder infections, respiratory problems and joint conditions. A large cage with enough room to play and exercise can help keep your guinea pig to stay in shape and ensure that they live a richer, healthier and better life.

Guinea pigs however, do not need the same exercise provisions as other small rodents such as hamsters and gerbils. They will be happy enough to run around in a large enclosure with one or two simple toys for the times when they are most active. Ensure they have lots of shade/ cover to shy away in if frightened, or seeking security. If you don't give your guinea pig enough things to entertain itself, it will be inactive and as a result, becoming bored and unhappy. **An active pet is a happy pet!**

28. Accessorize

Different guinea pigs like different types of toys; some will love one type, while others will simply ignore it.

It is good to experiment and give them a variety or different types of toy, most of which they will ignore but persist until you find something that entertains your particular pet. Usually the simpler the toy the better.

Guinea pig favorites are: *A toilet paper tube | a medium sized cardboard box | willow balls | plastic animal ball with bell | hanging fruit wood toys | a straw basket*

Change the toys, houses, and locations of toys frequently to keep things fresh and interesting for your pet. Keep toys, and especially houses and food dishes away from the walls and corners of the cage as they tend to use certain corner of the hutch as their toilet. Always ensure that the walls of the cage are clear to allow them room to exercise *(they will use this space to run around the perimeter)*.

29. Play

In their natural environment guinea pigs are quite active and playful little animals who love to engage themselves in games either on their own or with one of their companions.

Pet guinea pigs are no different and retain these basic instincts for playing. They often like to play on their own and they will happily amuse themselves with simple toys *(see above)*. Guinea pigs especially love to play with one another. Paper bags are ideal for guinea pigs to play with, chew on and have fun with.

Grooming

30. Grooming your guinea pig

Grooming requires daily attention. It is important that you take good care of your new pet to ensure that it is clean and healthy.

Guinea pigs molt constantly because of temperature changes and from grooming, so regular brushing ensures that their coat is always at its best.

Guinea pigs love to groom themselves, but they will certainly appreciate regular grooming from you too. This will also help in the bonding process with your new pet.

It is important that the rough/ long haired varieties of guinea pig are brushed regularly and their hair is kept in a good condition. They are prone to their hair becoming matted and knotted and this can become quite unpleasant and painful for your guinea pig if left unchecked. With long haired breeds, it is best to groom them daily to prevent this. It will also give you an ideal opportunity to check your guinea pig for anything out of the ordinary that could indicate a health issue. Obviously if you are unsure of anything you find, consult your vet.

To groom your guinea pig you will need a:

Brush: Soft pin brush is best.

Comb: A flea comb is best for smooth short coated varieties, although you may need a wider toothed barber comb for a longer haired variety.

Nail trimmer: Guillotine type or human kind can work as well (*see Top tips*).

Top tips

Trimming nails

We recommend you take your guinea pig to the vet for nail trimming.

However, in time and with the relative experience you may find that you can do it yourself. Although, it is advised that you first speak to a veterinary surgeon who can guide you through the technique of nail trimming.

IMPORTANT: there is part within the nail called the *'quick'* which is a vein and where the blood vessels and nerve endings are located. If you do accidently cut into the *quick* you will cause bleeding as well as considerable pain to you pet. The aim is to clip just the sharp tip of the nail without damaging the *quick*.

Guinea facts!

A great way to tame you new little pet is to offer a small amount of parsley for your guinea pig to munch on. Many guinea pigs find the sweet taste too tempting to ignore and will eagerly take it from you.

Health

31. Good health

To ensure your guinea pig remains in good health, make sure that their diet has an adequate intake of vitamins and minerals, through a fresh and high quality diet *(see p10)*.

1. Various gnaws are available from pets stores.

32. Wood gnaws

Wood gnaws are available in pet shops or you can provide your own by supplying the guinea pig with a piece of unsprayed fruit branch or untreated wood block to gnaw on.

These will provide the guinea pig with something on which to keep its teeth nice and trim. It would be a good idea to age the branches if you choose to use them. The drying process is extremely important as some of these branches are poisonous while fresh.

33. Health checks

Here are a couple of easy health checks that you can do yourself whilst your pet is sitting on your lap.

Check through your guinea pig's coat by running the tip of your finger against the lay of the hair to see if there is any dry skin or bald spots which may be indicative of a fungal or parasitic skin condition.

Check that its teeth are not broken or loose.

Checks to see if the nose is dry, the eyes are bright and that the guinea pig's movements are urgent and vigorous *(see p7)*.

Did you know?

Did you know the word *'rodent'* is derived from the Latin word *'rodere'* which means *'to gnaw'*.

34. Health problems

→→ Constipation or diarrhoea
This should be taken very seriously, they can both be caused by a bad diet or illness. Consult a vet if you have any queries.

→→ Parasites
Scratching is a common symptom of a skin complaint caused by parasites like *lice, mites* and *fleas*. Guinea pigs are usually free from parasites, but should your pet get an infestation, treat with a specialized medicated shampoo, mild insecticide powder or small animal '*Spot On*' drops. The most common type of parasite is the '*Seasonal static hay mite*' this particular mite is very difficult to see and only causes a problem when the infestation becomes large and your guinea pig scratches continuously. At first sign of any kind of parasite begin treatment.

→→ Respiratory infections
Guinea pigs are prone to respiratory infections and will usually have very similar symptoms to that of the of the human common cold. However, it can have a more serious impact on guinea pigs and should not be left untreated as it can lead to pneumonia. Keep your guinea pig out of damp environments and if the symptoms continue, consult your vet for further advice.

→→ Vitamin C deficiency
Guinea pigs cannot create their own vitamin C. A guinea pig suffering from vitamin deficiency will have a poor appetite and swollen, painful joints and chest. Conditions such as '*scurvy*' and '*displacer*' if left untreated it can be fatal. See a vet immediately.

→→ Eye injuries
These are very common in guinea pigs and indeed all hutch animals. Usually caused by hay poking them in the eyes. A saline wash will flush the eye of any foreign bodies but consult your vet if problems persist.

→→ Worms
Guinea pigs are affected by both *roundworms* and *tapeworms*. Symptoms include a distended abdomen, poor coat and worms in the feces. Other things to look out for are lethargy, a dull or uneven coat, and a crouching posture.

Top tips

Heat exhaustion

Animals confined to small, badly ventilated hutches or left in direct sunlight from which they cannot escape can be affected by heat exhaustion. If an animal is found in obvious distress, its back must be wetted immediately with a damp cloth and moved to a cool place with good ventilation. It should be fanned if severely affected.

✔

→→ Fly strike
Usually found in elderly, infirm and long-haired guinea pigs at the end of the summer. Caused by the blow fly laying eggs in feces-soiled fur. Within 24 hours, larvae hatch out and eat their way into the guinea pigs rectum. You should check your pets daily to ensure their coats are free from feces.

• • • • • • • • • • • • • • • •

Other things to look out for aside from the health issues mentioned are lethargy, a dull or uneven coat, and a crouching posture. *If you think one of your guinea pigs is ill, take your pet to a qualified vet.*

Hutch care

35. Home sweet home

A covering is required for the floor of the cage to provide a soft, comfortable surface for the guinea pig and also to soak up the urine.

The most common type of floor covering available is wood shavings. Fine sawdust should be avoided as this can cause irritation to the eyes and to the lungs.

Cedar wood shavings *(usually distinguished by a red tint)* should not be used as the *phenols* they contain can cause severe irritation. Although pine is also a softwood, **pine wood shavings** cause less problems than cedar and **kiln dried pine** can be used without problems.

You should steer clear of any scented shavings such as lemon and lavender as these can cause irritation to your guinea pig. Corn cob bedding is not generally recommended as it has a tendency to mold and guinea pigs have been known to eat it which is a problem as it can swell when wet inside the stomach.

Wood shavings from hardwoods such as aspen or small animal litter made from wood pulp are the safest forms of floor covering to use.

36. Timothy hay & alfalfa hay

Guinea pigs need roughage in the form of either of these hays. They can be obtained from any local pet shop.

Do not buy hay that is damp as this can be moldy and dangerous for your guinea pig. Keep it stored in a dry, cool place.

These types of hay are suitable although *timothy* or standard meadow hays are the favored choices as *alfalfa* is already included in guinea pig pellets and can be a contributing factor to some guinea pigs becoming overweight.

1.

Top tips

Chirping

On occasion, you may hear one of you guinea pigs making calling sounds similar to bird song.

This behavior is called *'chirping'* No one has been able to explain this rare and beautiful behavior. Some believe that it is a form of expressing total joy, because when they perform this, any other guinea pig will lie down and listen intently while the chirper lifts one paw and rocks their head almost trance like. While others say it is a claim to dominance of the group.

✔

Important!

Straw should not be used as the sharp edges can injure a guinea pig eyes. Alfalfa hay is considered too high in calcium for continued use throughout adulthood, although it can be given as an occasional treat.

1. Kiln-dried pine shavings.
2. Two storey hutch.

2.

Top tips

Bathing

You must always be careful when bathing your guinea pig.

Unlike most other small animals, a guinea pig does not have a reflex to hold their breath when under water, so always make sure that the water level is never higher than their chins.

✔

37. Hutch cleaning

It is said that guinea pigs are odorless which is true to an extent, however, even an odorless pets hutch will smell if it isn't cleaned for an extended period. Urine soaked bedding, feces and decaying vegetable matter all make your pets' hutch an unpleasant place to live and encourage flies and other undesired pests to take hold.

Outdoor hutches in particular get unhygienic very quickly, and to keep your guinea pigs environment clean and healthy you will need to make sure that you are cleaning it out regularly *(everyday if in constant use by multiple guinea pigs)*.

Remove your guinea pigs and make sure you place them in a safe and secure place before you begin cleaning their hutch *(a guinea pig/ rabbit run is ideal whilst cleaning)*.

Once a day you should remove all droppings.

Check that the bedding and hutch litter is dry *(as damp conditions are bad for guinea pigs)*.

Tidy the sleeping area and ensure that they have fresh clean water and the bottle is free of algae *(use a mild animal safe detergent once a week to clean the water bottle, rinse thoroughly and replace with fresh water in the hutch)*.

Once a week, clean the whole hutch using a sturdy brush and good animal-friendly cleaning disinfectant *(Wait until the inside of the hutch is completely dry before replacing the litter and bedding and putting your guinea pig back in)*.

Handling your guinea pig

38. Gently does it

Guinea pigs are shy animals but they are also very simple animals to handle. Initially, they may not enjoy being lifted at all. They will need to be taught gradually from a young age to tolerate being picked up, as it is an important part of caring for your guinea pig.

In the beginning get your guinea pig used to you by feeding it bits of vegetable or fruit from your hand and talking softly to them, using their name frequently. In time it will become used to this and will let you stroke it whilst it is feeding. Don't worry if it does not become accustomed to this straight away, be patient and allow your pet to become comfortable with you. Once you have achieved this you will be able to go on to the next stage.

When picking up a guinea pig, approach them slowly, and only from the front. They are easily startled and are certain to run for cover if they feel like they are being stalked by a predator. Try to keep them calm throughout the process by talking gently to your guinea pig whilst gently stroking it. Once you have gained its trust, place one hand firmly on its back *(not too firmly as you don't want to damage their fragile bones and organs)* and place the remaining hand under the guinea pig, just behind the front feet, and use your other hand to support its back end. Bring it in close to your chest continuing to support it using both hands, one supporting its back end and the other placed over the shoulders. Always lift your pet with smooth and gentle movements as not to scare it. If you are new to guinea pigs or have one that really struggles, then you should kneel on the floor to lift them up, this will minimize the chance of any injury should your guinea pig wriggle free from your grasp. They are fragile creatures and can suffer greatly if dropped, even if from a short height.

39. Small children & safety

Children should be sat down *(preferably on the floor)*, when you pass the guinea pig to them.

Teach them to be gentle and to only stroke the hair in the direction the hair is growing. When placing your guinea pigs back in their cage, they can become quite excited, so be extra careful not to drop them. Try to release your hold on them only once they are safely on the ground.

Important!
Never pick a guinea pig up with one hand around the back of the neck and rib cage. Your guinea pig will find this very frightening as though it has been caught by a predator.

40. Stroking

If your guinea pig doesn't want you to stroke its head, it will let you know in the form of throwing its head upwards or pushing away the hand that strokes it.

It is wise to honor its wishes and stop stroking it when it does this. It either means he doesn't like being stroked there or is bored of it. Ignoring this will only hinder the bonding process and could result in a light bite.

41. Vocalizations

→ **Squealing:** Pain, fear, loneliness or begging for food.

→ **Cooing:** A Soothing, calming sound made from a mother to her young, but is also used for adult friends as well. You may be treated to cooing from your guinea pig if you have a close bond and it feels comfortable with you.

→ **Rattling, hissing, teeth chattering:** Aggression, warning or sometimes trying to impress a female.

→ **Murmurs, gurgles & grunts:** Contentment, comfort much like a cats purr. It is a sign of your guinea pigs happiness.

Top tips

Sociable

Guinea pigs have a highly social nature and it is not recommended that you keep them as solitary pets.

Regardless of how much attention you give them, they will still suffer from loneliness, especially if kept alone in an outdoor hutch.

You will need to make special efforts to provide social interaction. Bringing your guinea pig into the house as often as possible will enable it to spend time with you. Sitting with your guinea pig in the garden as it plays in its run from time to time is also a good idea, however it is still recommended that you get another guinea pig friend to keep them company in their hutch.

Know your guinea pig

42. Guinea pig anatomy

The anatomy of the guinea pig is the result of years of evolution and shows the adaptations it has had to undertake to survive.

Their body is designed for its main tasks, eating, reproducing and fleeing from predators. Their heightened senses and ability to spot danger early and run for cover is the reason that the species flourished. Other Cavies of note are; *Capybara, Degu, Kerodon Acrobata, Tapir* and the *Rock Cavy* to name a few.

Adult guinea pigs weigh between two and three pounds and measure about 10 inches *(25 cm)* long. It has a short, stocky body, large eyes and no visible tail. The front feet are flat and have four digits with claws. The hind feet have three digits with claws and are much longer than the front ones.

Stroking

All guinea pigs like to be stroked in different places. Some like to be tickled underneath the chin, others behind the ears and some even like their bellies to be gently stroked. Try to find your pets' favorite spot.

43. Guinea pig behavior

→ Touching noses, nuzzling

Greeting & acknowledgement. Reserved for familiar friends. You can show affection to your own guinea pig by gently rubbing noses with it. It will most likely gently lick you or carefully study your face.

→ Jumping

Jumping straight up in the air is known as *'popcorning',* and is a typical display of joy.

→ Sitting up or standing

Begging for food.

→ Lowering the head, growling

Fear, submissive, offering of peace.

→ Mouth wide open, showing teeth

Female rejecting male's advances, males displaying to one another as a warning.

→ Stretching the head forwards

Watchful and alert.

→ Retracting legs under body and backed up against a wall

Helpless and scared, needing protection.

→ Turning rigid

Your guinea pig is *'playing dead'* in order to disarm what it sees as a threat in an attempt to disarm a predators attack. If you guinea pig does this, it is likely that it is scared. It would be kind to reassure it or take it out of the scary situation that it has found itself in.

→ Out-stretched

An out-stretched posture is a relaxed one in guinea pigs. It is a sign that it is comfortable in its surroundings and able to relax.

→ Stress

Guinea pigs are susceptible to stress much like humans, although unlike us, they have no way of changing their lives to make it better for themselves. Stress will impact on your pets' immune system and can adversely affect its ability to fight off infections. Keep your guinea pig away from extreme temperatures, out of noisy environments and away from intimidating animals/people. To relieve stress make sure your guinea pig is well exercised and has plenty of company.

→ Hair stripping

A curious behavior where your guinea pig may start to strip and clip the hair from its body and/or their hutch mates. This is most commonly caused by boredom, or brought on by inactivity and a lack of gnawing toys. However, long haired varieties do cut their own hair if it is getting to long from time to time. If you are concerned about their health, take them to your vet for a check-up.

Breeding advice

44. Golden rules for breeding

Before even considering breeding guinea pigs, it is best to make sure that you can find homes for the inevitable litter!

It is important to know that your guinea pigs will reach sexual maturity very quickly indeed, and if you wish to avoid offspring, you must keep the male guinea pigs separated from the females.

Companions

Male *(boar)* Guinea pigs make great companions with female *(sow)* guinea pigs and will often be seen kissing their partner and dotting on them by passing tasty food treats to her.

If you do plan on keeping a male and female together, it will be quite likely that you will have baby guinea pigs to deal with at some point. It's important you decide early on, whether you intend to breed or not.

Where guinea pigs are concerned you need to be especially careful. They are difficult to sex so it is vital that you know whether or not you are keeping a same sex pair *(p6)*.

45. Mini-pigs

Guinea pigs give birth to fully furred babies with their eyes wide open. Soon after birth they are fully functional, running around and exploring their surroundings.

It is very important that you keep the male away from the female in this initial period because he will mate with her immediately after birth and two pregnancies so close to one another can cause a massive strain on the sow.

"Did you know, A group of guinea pigs is called a Clutch?"

46. Preparing the cage

If you decide to breed your own guinea pigs you should prepare the cage with the little guinea pigs in mind.

They are little more than the size of a *Syrian* hamster at this stage, so food bowls and water bottles must be at a height that the new born guinea pigs can reach. The mother should have plenty of hay to create her birthing nest. She will also need extra food and water both before and after the birth, which will normally take place in the evening in a private area of the hutch. Guinea pigs are kind and devoted mothers and will look after their young intently. Provide her and her babies with a place to hide away and nurse.

47. Introductions

You may decide to introduce a new guinea pig to an existing one you already own. Guinea pigs are by nature social and agreeable little creatures. However, introductions can be a tricky process.

Females tend to take to a new friend easier than males, though any introduction must be done slowly and with care. One method is to place your new guinea pigs cage next to your existing pets and swap the bedding to and from the cages on a daily basis until they become familiar with each others scent. Allow them to run together in a neutral surrounding for short periods and then eventually place them together in a cage. It is worth mentioning however that any new introduction must be with a younger guinea pig, preferably under 4 months of age. An older guinea pig will vie for position with your existing pet, leading to possible injury and emotional distress.

Signs to watch for when introducing are:

Rumble strutting - Your guinea pigs will rock back and forth, grumbling and teeth chattering, rolling their bottoms towards each other.

Scenting - You may notice a strong musty sweet smell, this is normal and part of the territorial marking.

Tail lifting - One guinea pig will chase the other, lifting the others rump with their nose, they do this to sniff the scent glands of the other guinea pig

Vibrating - One guinea pig may jump on top of the other and vibrate and scent them, this is to show the other who is the boss and in charge.

If this behavior goes on for more than 48 hours the introduction unfortunately may not work and you will need to separate the pair.

Top tips

Pregnant sows

The average size litter is three but it can be bigger so be prepared *(see p4).*

Pregnant sows will need extra food and double rations of vitamin C. This can be found in fruit and vegetables or additional supplements *(see p11).*

Titles in series

Magnet & Steel Ltd
Unit 6
Vale Business Park,
Llandow, United Kingdom. CF71 7PF
sales@magnetsteel.com
www.magnetsteel.com